EARLY TO LATER ELEMENTARY

FAVORITE
FESTIVAL ENSEMBLES

8 GREAT NFMC SELECTIONS

The **National Federation of Music Clubs (NFMC)** is a non-profit philanthropic music organization whose goal is to promote American music, performers, and composers through quality music education and to support the highest standards of musical creativity and performance.

CONTENTS

ISBN 978-1-4584-1772-5

EXCLUSIVELY DISTRIBUTED BY

WILLIS MUSIC   HAL•LEONARD®

Visit Hal Leonard Online at
www.halleonard.com

World headquarters, contact:
Hal Leonard
7777 West Bluemound Road
Milwaukee, WI 53213
Email: info@halleonard.com

In Europe, contact:
Hal Leonard Europe Limited
1 Red Place
London, W1K 6PL
Email: info@halleonardeurope.com

In Australia, contact:
Hal Leonard Australia Pty. Ltd.
4 Lentara Court
Cheltenham, Victoria, 3192 Australia
Email: info@halleonard.com.au

ON THE TRAIL / Carolyn Miller
NFMC 2004-2006

Note from Carolyn Miller: Play this duet with energy! Note that the Primo plays an octave higher than written and the Secondo an octave lower—the intent was to make this a "full" sounding duet. The piece is in ABA form with a Coda, and both parts take turns with the melody. Imagine the A section as someone happily singing or humming while walking on the trail, and accompanied by light staccatos in the Secondo. The duet is easily put together and fun to play!

ROCK-A-BYE FIVE / Marian Hall
NFMC 1998-2000

Think dreamy, legato lines when playing this piece. The 1st and 2nd Players start the piece with a pretty duet in perfect 4ths, and the 3rd Player provides a steady, solid rocking motion in the bass. Watch the phrase marks carefully; it would be a good idea to coordinate the phrasing as a group before performing.

[To the teacher: This would make an excellent first recital piece for a trio of early level beginners—less intimidating for the performers, and fun for the audience!]

THE OLD-TIME FIDDLER / Dorothy Gaynor Blake
NFMC 1991-1994

Dorothy Gaynor Blake (1893-1967) was a composer, singer and pianist from Missouri who published over 800 pieces in her lifetime. "The Old-Time Fiddler" was written way back in 1929, and yet it could easily have been written today. It sounds just like its title—fast and lively; you can picture a violinist happily improvising in a casual setting. Notice the introduction: all four open strings on a violin are showcased! The Secondo is important, too: it provides the solid foundation throughout the piece. Practice this piece with your partner slowly at first; then work it up to a steady, vigorous, foot-stomping tempo.

CHIAPANECAS / Arr. Edna Mae Burnam
NFMC 1991-1994

Get ready for some fun at the piano! You (and your teacher) will probably recognize this traditional tune immediately—it's also known as the "Mexican Hand-Clapping Song"—and yes, both Primo and Secondo will have their share of hand claps while playing! Practice with a metronome to make sure that your hand claps are right on the beat, and check that there is no hesitation after the claps to find the correct hand position once again.

P.S. Edna Mae Burnam (1907-2007) lived to be almost a century old and was a pioneer in the world of piano pedagogy. Odds are that you've practiced out of one of her best-selling technique books! (Do stick figures ring a bell?)

SONG WITHOUT WORDS / David Karp
NFMC 1995-1997

Note from David Karp: The Primo sings this song (*cantabile*) without words as the Secondo accompanies with repeated chords and damper pedal (the pedal on the right). Listen to the singing melody in the Primo part and be sure that the Secondo plays softer so that the melody is always heard. Also, listen to the Secondo part's pedaling to be sure there are no "blurs." Notice the dynamic markings at the beginning: *mp* for Primo and *p* for Secondo. Does Secondo play any melody, and if so, in which measures?

THE STAR SPANGLED BANNER / Arr. Mark Nevin
NFMC 1981-1982

This American favorite has a well-deserved reputation of being difficult to sing; luckily, it is much easier to play as a duet on the piano! Although the Primo carries the melody for the whole song, the Secondo joins in unison in several significant places. Find those distinctive places in the music before you begin practicing. And, remember to listen to each other after the fermata in M.28, so you can both build effectively towards an impressive and majestic end.

MARCH OF THE JUMPING-JACKS / Mathilde Bilbro
NFMC 1991-1994

This piece may be played by 3 people on 1 piano, or 6 people on 2 pianos. It would be a good idea to choose a "leader"—the person with the best rhythm—who will set the tempo of the piece before starting. (Or, everyone can take turns at being the "leader.")

A "jumping-jack" is a wooden toy that originated in Egypt and was once very popular in Europe and the United States. It is similar to a puppet or figurine. The flexible arms and legs are connected by a string: when the string is pulled, the jumping-jack moves! As you practice and perform this piece with your ensemble partners, imagine a line of little, magical jumping-jacks marching together in strict time.

PEACE PIPE / David Karp
NFMC 2004-2006

Note from David Karp: This duet is in the key of A Minor. The Secondo's left hand plays a steady drum beat, the right hand plays lots of grace notes called *acciaccaturas* (which mean "crushed"). The Primo has the main melody in the right hand, the left hand provides an accompanying third. Does the Primo's left hand always play thirds? Take a look and tell your teacher where it changes. A fast tempo and exciting dynamics will make this an energetic performance. Listen closely as the music fades away at the end.

On the Trail

SECONDO

Play both hands one octave lower.

Carolyn Miller

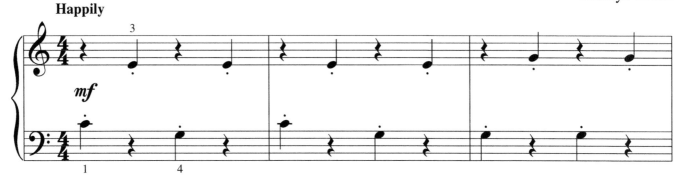

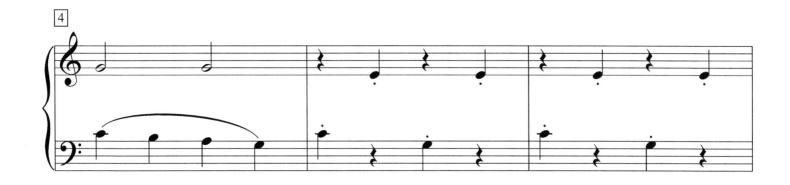

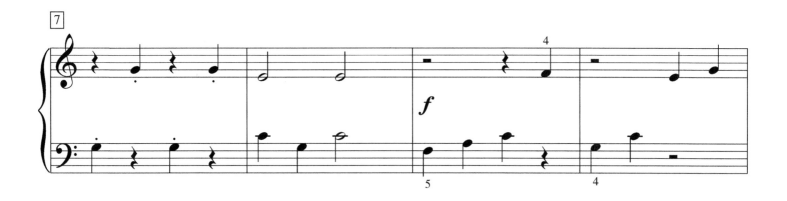

On the Trail

PRIMO

Play both hands one octave higher.

Carolyn Miller

Happily

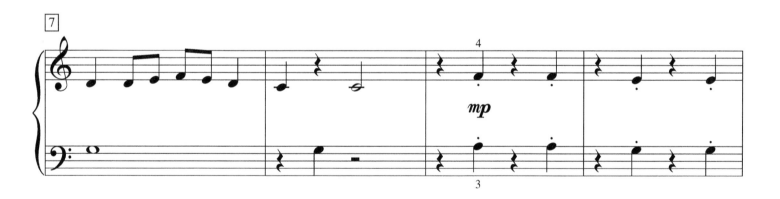

PRIMO

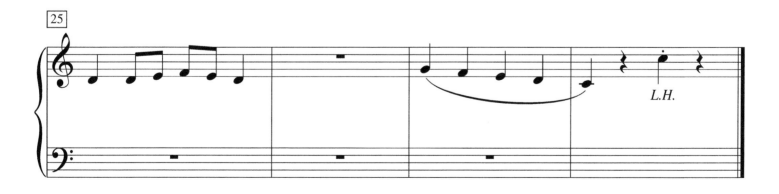

Rock-A-Bye Five
One Piano, Six Hands

3RD PLAYER
Left Hand Solo

Marian Hall

TEACHER'S SCORE (Parts Combined)

Rock-A-Bye Five
One Piano, Six Hands

1ST PLAYER
Right Hand Solo

Marian Hall

(Play an octave higher than written.)
Moderato, dreamy

2ND PLAYER
Right Hand Solo

Marian Hall

Moderato, dreamy

The Old-Time Fiddler

SECONDO

Dorothy Gaynor Blake
(1893–1967)

Fast and lively

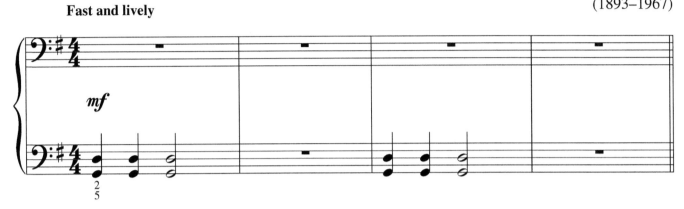

The Old-Time Fiddler

PRIMO

Dorothy Gaynor Blake
(1893–1967)

Fast and lively

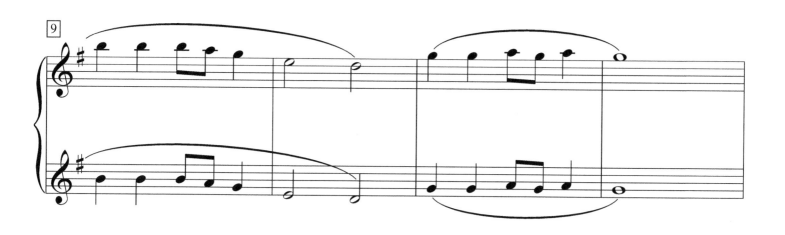

SECONDO

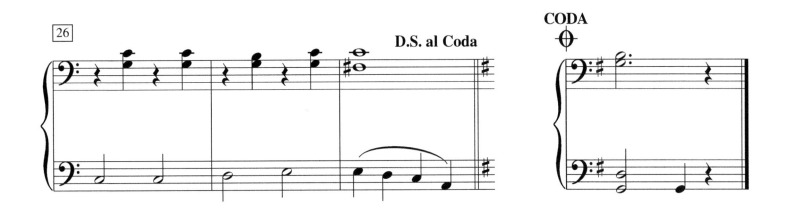

PRIMO

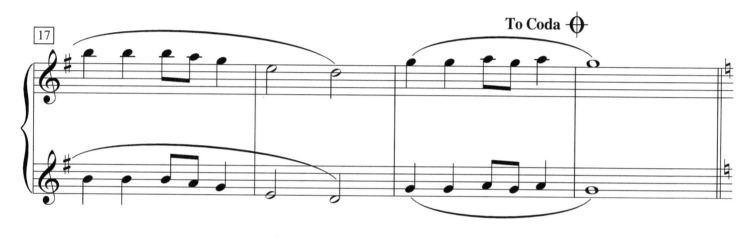

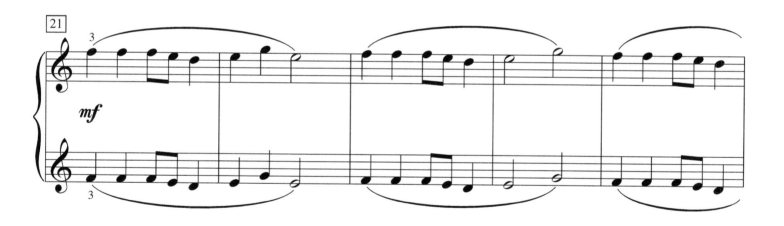

Chiapanecas

SECONDO

Traditional
Arranged by Edna Mae Burnam
(1907–2007)

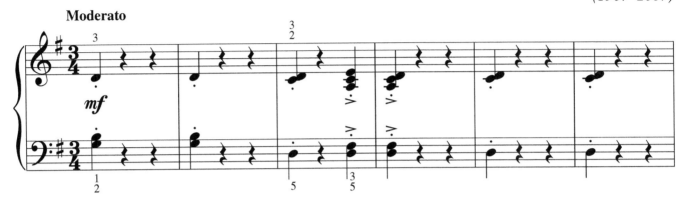

*Clap hands!

Chiapanecas

PRIMO

Traditional
Arranged by Edna Mae Burnam
(1907–2007)

Moderato
Play R.H. one octave higher throughout.

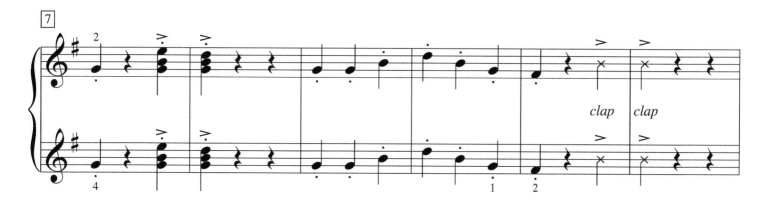

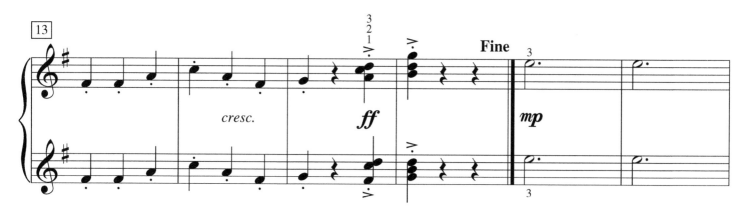

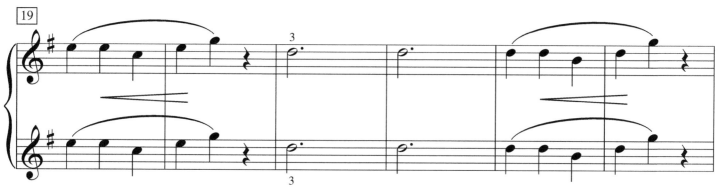

*Clap hands!

SECONDO

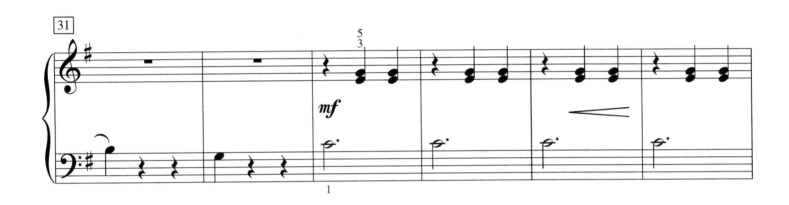

D.C. al Fine

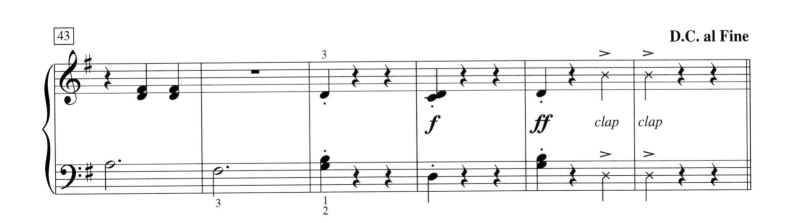

PRIMO

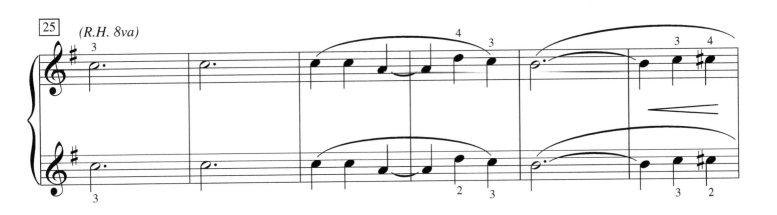

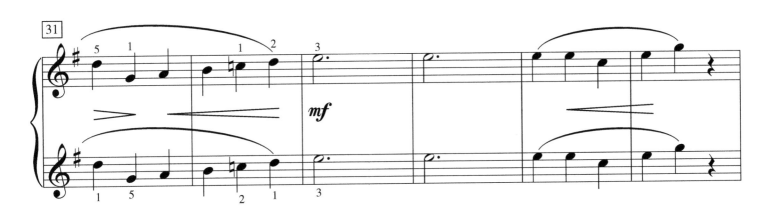

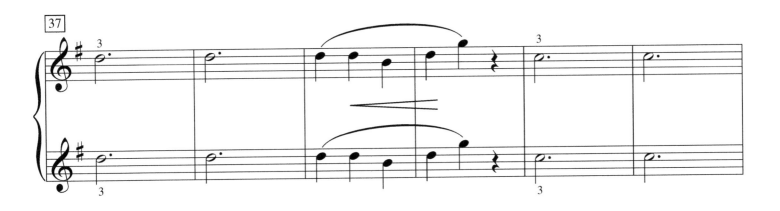

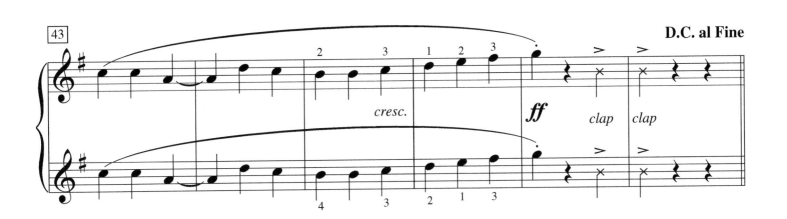

The Star Spangled Banner

SECONDO

Words by Francis Scott Key
Music by John Stafford Smith
Arranged by Mark Nevin

The Star Spangled Banner

PRIMO

Words by Francis Scott Key
Music by John Stafford Smith
Arranged by Mark Nevin

SECONDO

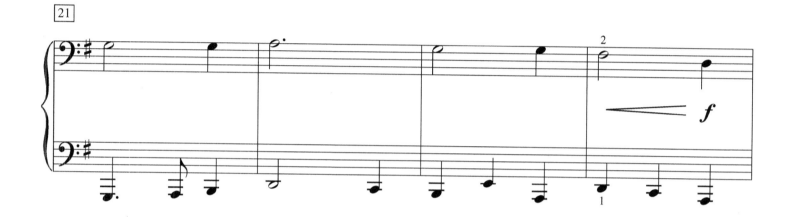

PRIMO

To Grey Geller Golman
Song Without Words

SECONDO

David Karp

To Grey Geller Golman

Song Without Words

PRIMO

David Karp

SECONDO

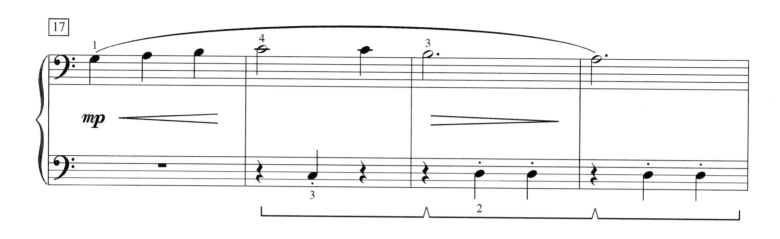

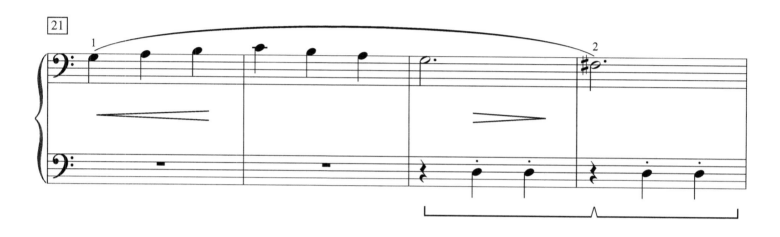

D.C. al Fine

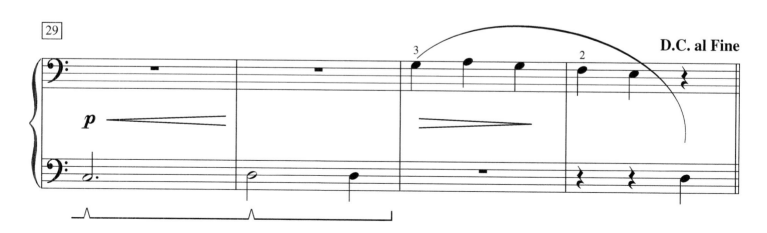

PRIMO

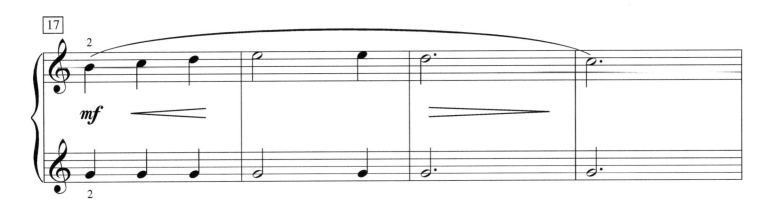

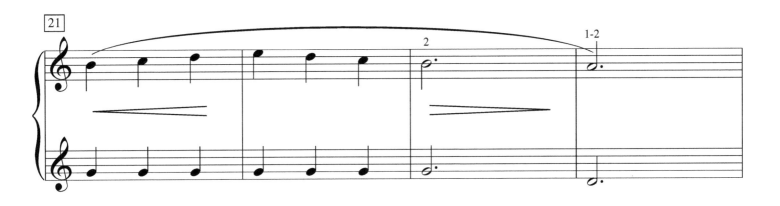

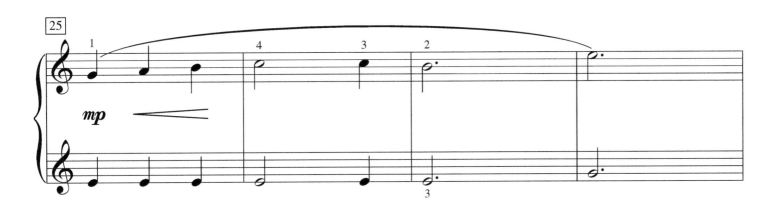

D.C. al Fine

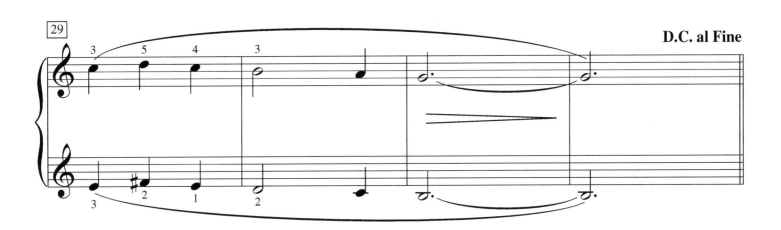

March of the Jumping-Jacks

One Piano, Six Hands
(or Two Pianos, Twelve Hands)

3RD PLAYER

Mathilde Bilbro
(1870–1958)

March of the Jumping-Jacks

One Piano, Six Hands
(or Two Pianos, Twelve Hands)

1ST PLAYER

Mathilde Bilbro
(1870–1958)

*Both hands

2ND PLAYER

Mathilde Bilbro
(1870–1958)

To Brady Asher Karp

Peace Pipe

SECONDO

David Karp

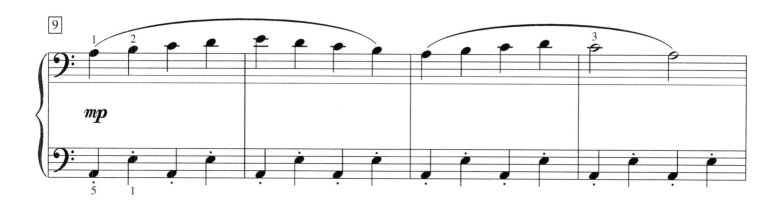

To Brady Asher Karp

Peace Pipe

PRIMO

David Karp

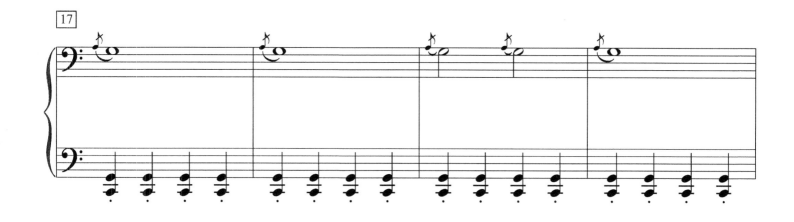

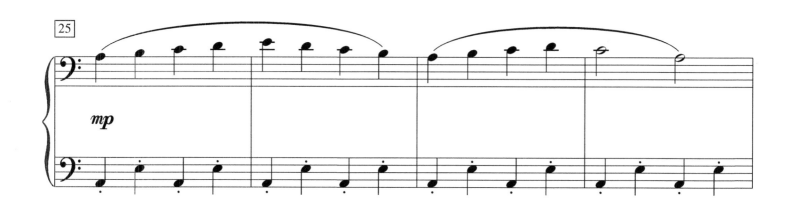

PRIMO

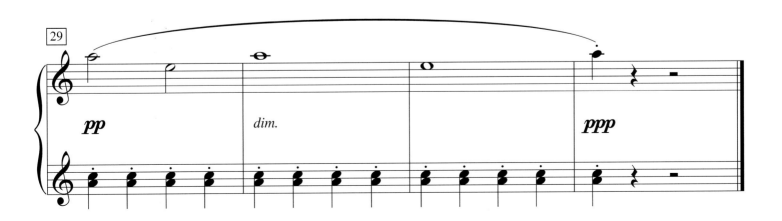

Also Available

Favorite Festival Ensembles, Book 2

8 More NFMC Duets and Trios:
The Chase (Miller/Engle) • Kibbutz Capers (Karp) • Oriental Bazaar (Gillock)
• Petite Spanish Dance (Miller) • Pinwheels (Beard) • Polka (Karp) • Trepak
(Tchaikovsky, arr. Gillock) • Western Bolero (Karp).